HOW TO LIVE RICH

WHEN YOUR BANK ACCOUNT SAYS YOU'RE POOR

By Mylia Tiye Mal Jaza

To those who have been counted out, overlooked,
tuckered from the struggle of the
check-to-check rat race, and underestimated.
May you discover that wealth was
never something you had to wait for,
as you remember and radiate this fact:
"Being rich is not just about what you
have in your possession. It is how you move,
how you see, how you adjust,
and how you live freely."

How To Live Rich When Your Bank Account Says You're Poor

Written By

Mylia Tiye Mal Jaza

Fullcover Design By

Sun Child Wind Spirit

Proofread By

Kathrina Goode-Long

How To Live Rich When Your Bank Account Says You're Poor

Softcover ISBN-10: 9656227263

Softcover ISBN-13: 9783517385938

Author Contact
Mylia Tiye Mal Jaza
Chicago, Illinois
c/o The Writers Consortium
writersconsortium@bepublished.biz

Self-Publishing Associate
BePublished.Org - Chicago
(972) 880-8316
P.O. Box 8324
Jackson, MS 39284
www.bepublished.org
publisher@bepublished.org

First Edition.
Printed In the USA.
Recycled Paper Encouraged.

THE WRITERS CONSORTIUM
www.WritersConsortium.us

TABLE OF CONTENT

(MORE)

TOC (cont'd)

(###)

INTRODUCTION

You Were Never Poor, Just Taught By Society To Feel That Way

There is a particular kind of silence that settles into a life when money is tight. It does not always announce itself loudly, nor does it need to. It lingers in the background of daily decisions, shaping what you say yes to and what you quietly deny yourself.

It shows up in the hesitation before a purchase, in the mental calculations that accompany even the smallest indulgences, and in the subtle but persistent feeling that life is happening just outside of your reach.

I have known that silence intimately. I have sat with it long enough to understand that it is not merely about numbers in a bank account. It is about the way those numbers begin to speak, and more importantly, the authority we give them. Over time, what begins as a financial limitation can evolve into something far more insidious — a belief system that tells you who you are, what you deserve, and how much of life you are allowed to experience.

The danger is not in having limited resources. The danger is in allowing those limitations to define your identity. When that happens, scarcity stops being a condition and becomes a lens through which everything is viewed.

You begin to move differently, to shrink your expectations, and to postpone joy as though it were a luxury reserved only for some future version of yourself. Without realizing it, you start living as if life must be earned in advance, rather than experienced in the present.

This book exists to interrupt that pattern. It is not written to dismiss the realities of financial struggle, nor to pretend that money is irrelevant. Money has its place, and its absence can create very real challenges. However, what this book insists upon is the understanding that wealth, in its truest form, has never been confined to currency.

There are people with vast financial resources who live in constant dissatisfaction, and there are those with modest means who carry a depth of peace, clarity, and fulfillment that cannot be purchased or replicated.

The difference between these experiences is not access, but awareness. It is the ability to recognize that a rich life is not something postponed until conditions are perfect, but something constructed through intention, discipline, and perspective. When you begin to see wealth as a way of being rather than a number to be reached, you reclaim a level of control that no external circumstance can take from you.

Living rich does not require denial of your current reality; it requires mastery of how you engage with it. It calls for a shift in how you define value, how you allocate your time and energy, and how you treat yourself in moments when no one else is watching. It asks you to develop standards that are not dependent on income, and to cultivate a mindset that refuses to equate temporary financial limitation with permanent personal lack.

If you cannot access a sense of richness with what you have now, more will not solve that absence. It will only magnify it. On the other hand, if you learn to live with intention, clarity, and self-respect in this season, you create a foundation that will support you regardless of what your financial future holds.

This book blows no smoke up your skirt and doesn't encourage you to pretending to be wealthy. It is about becoming someone who understands wealth deeply enough to live it, even before it is reflected externally. It is about recognizing that richness is expressed in how you think, how you move, and how you experience your life on a daily basis.

You were never poor in the way you were taught to believe. You were conditioned to measure yourself by a system that was never designed to capture your full value.

This book will help you unlearn that conditioning and replace it with something far more powerful: a deliberate, grounded, and unshakable way of living that allows you to experience richness now, not someday.

And once you understand that, every single solitary thing begins to change. You might even find yourself playing a game of "Reverse Psychology With The Universe."

CHAPTER ONE

The Lie About Being Broke

The word *broke* carries a weight that extends far beyond its financial definition. It is not merely descriptive; it is suggestive. It implies damage, limitation, and in many cases, a quiet sense of failure. Over time, it begins to attach itself not just to circumstances, but to identity.

People do not simply say, "I have less money right now."

Instead, they say, "I am broke," and in doing so, they collapse a temporary condition into a permanent self-concept.

This distinction matters more than most people realize. When a financial state becomes an identity, it begins to shape behavior in ways that reinforce the very condition one hopes to escape. Decisions become smaller.

Expectations become lower. Possibilities are filtered through a lens of assumed limitation. What begins as a shortage of money slowly transforms into a shortage of vision, and from there, into a pattern of living that feels confined, even when opportunities are present.

Much of this conditioning is inherited rather than chosen. From an early age, many people are taught — directly or indirectly — that money dictates access, and access dictates experience. The narrative is repeated in subtle ways: you will enjoy life later, you will travel when you can afford it, you will invest in yourself when you are more stable. Until then, you are expected to wait. Waiting becomes normalized, and eventually, it becomes a habit so deeply ingrained that it is rarely questioned.

The problem with this way of thinking is not that it acknowledges financial reality, but that it grants that reality too much authority. It assumes that life must be postponed until conditions improve, and in doing so, it overlooks the vast number of ways in which richness can be experienced independently of income. Time, attention, discipline, creativity, and perspective all contribute to the quality of one's life, yet they are often undervalued because they are not easily measured in currency.

There is also a quieter, more subtle consequence of identifying as broke, and it reveals itself in the standards a person is willing to accept. When someone believes they are operating from a place of lack, they often tolerate environments, relationships, and habits that do not reflect their true worth.

Clutter is excused. Disrespect is overlooked. Time is wasted. Energy is misallocated. These choices are rarely framed as significant, yet they accumulate, gradually shaping a life that feels heavy, disorganized, and disconnected from any sense of abundance.

Living poor, in this sense, is not always about the absence of money. It is often about the absence of intention. It is the result of repeatedly choosing what is easy over what is aligned, what is immediate over what is meaningful, and what is available over what is truly valuable. Over time, these patterns become familiar, and familiarity can be mistaken for inevitability.

To challenge this pattern requires a shift that is both simple and demanding. It begins with recognizing that your financial condition, while real, does not have the authority to define the quality of your life in its entirety. It requires you to separate circumstance from identity, and to see clearly where you have unconsciously allowed one to dictate the other. This awareness is not meant to minimize struggle, but to prevent it from becoming a permanent framework through which all decisions are made.

Once that separation is established, a different way of living becomes available. You begin to evaluate your choices through a new lens, one that prioritizes clarity, self-respect, and intentionality over automatic reactions to perceived lack.

You become more selective about where your time goes, more deliberate about how your environment is maintained, and more aware of the standards you uphold in both small and significant areas of your life.

This is where the concept of living rich begins to take form. It is not rooted in denial or illusion, but in a disciplined refusal to allow temporary financial limitations to erode your sense of worth or your commitment to a meaningful life.

It is expressed in how you carry yourself, how you structure your days, and how you engage with the world around you. It is visible in the consistency of your actions and the clarity of your priorities.

Over time, this way of living produces its own momentum. The decisions you make begin to align with a higher standard, and that alignment creates opportunities that may not have been visible before.

Your thinking expands, your expectations evolve, and your relationship with money itself begins to change.

Rather than viewing it as the sole determinant of what is possible, you begin to see it as one component within a broader system of value that you are actively shaping.

The lie about being broke is not that money is irrelevant, but that it is all-defining. Once you see that clearly, you are no longer confined by it.

You are free to build a life that reflects intention, discipline, and depth — one that feels rich not because of what it displays, but because of how it is lived. And that is where real wealth begins.

CHAPTER TWO

Wealth Without Permission

One of the most subtle, yet most damaging beliefs a person can carry is the idea that a rich life must be granted rather than created. It is the quiet assumption that there is an invisible threshold — financial, social, or professional — that must be crossed before one is allowed to experience ease, beauty, or fulfillment. Until that threshold is reached, life is treated as something to endure rather than something to inhabit fully.

This belief rarely presents itself in obvious ways. Instead, it appears in the small deferrals that shape daily life. You tell yourself you will take better care of your space when you move somewhere nicer, that you will invest in your health when you have more disposable income, or that you will pursue meaningful experiences when you are more financially secure. Each of these statements seems reasonable on the surface, yet together they form a pattern of postponement that quietly distances you from the very life you claim to want.

At its core, this pattern is not about money. It is about permission. It reflects an internalized hierarchy in which you place your current self beneath some imagined future version who is more deserving, more capable, and more entitled to live well. In doing so, you deny yourself access to richness in the present, as though it were a reward to be earned rather than a standard to be upheld.

The truth is that no external authority is responsible for granting you the right to live with intention, clarity, and self-respect. These are not privileges reserved for a select group of people; they are choices that remain available regardless of financial status. While money can expand options, it does not determine whether you treat your time as valuable, whether you maintain your environment with care, or whether you engage with your life in a way that reflects purpose.

Living without permission requires a deliberate shift in how you view your current circumstances. Instead of seeing them as a holding pattern, you begin to treat them as a foundation. Every decision you make becomes an opportunity to reinforce the kind of life you are building, rather than a reminder of what you lack. You stop waiting for ideal conditions and start working with what is already in front of you, recognizing that consistency in small actions often carries more weight than occasional bursts of effort fueled by temporary motivation.

This shift is particularly important when it comes to how you allocate your attention. Attention is one of the most valuable resources you possess, yet it is frequently given away without consideration. Hours are spent consuming content that does not elevate your thinking, engaging in conversations that do not contribute to your growth, or dwelling on limitations that do not move you forward. Over time, this pattern reinforces a sense of stagnation, making it feel as though progress is out of reach.

Reclaiming your attention is an act of quiet power. It allows you to direct your focus toward what is constructive, meaningful, and aligned with your values. When you begin to choose deliberately what you engage with, you create an environment — both internal and external — that supports a richer way of living. This does not require additional money; it requires awareness and discipline.

There is also a physical dimension to living without permission, and it is often overlooked. The way you carry yourself, the care you put into your appearance, and the condition of your immediate surroundings all communicate a standard, both to yourself and to others. When these elements are approached with intention, they create a sense of order and self-respect that is not dependent on wealth. A clean, organized space, thoughtful presentation, and a calm, deliberate presence can transform how you experience your daily life, even in modest circumstances.

Equally important is the way you relate to your own aspirations. Many people hesitate to pursue what they truly want because they believe they are not yet in the right position to do so. They wait for validation, for resources, or for some external signal that confirms they are ready. In the absence of that signal, they remain inactive, telling themselves that their time will come later.

Living rich without permission challenges this hesitation. It encourages you to engage with your aspirations now, in whatever capacity is available to you. This may mean starting small, learning gradually, or building incrementally, but it removes the illusion that action must be delayed until conditions are perfect. Progress becomes something you participate in continuously, rather than something you anticipate from a distance.

As you begin to operate from this perspective, your relationship with money itself starts to shift. Instead of viewing it as the sole determinant of what is possible, you begin to see it as a tool that interacts with a broader set of factors, including discipline, creativity, and consistency. This does not diminish the importance of financial growth, but it places it within a larger context, allowing you to recognize the areas where you already have influence.

Over time, living without permission cultivates a sense of stability that is not easily disrupted by external fluctuations. Because your standard of living is rooted in intention rather than circumstance, you are less dependent on temporary changes in income to feel secure or fulfilled. This does not mean that financial challenges disappear, but it does mean that they no longer dictate the entirety of your experience.

Ultimately, wealth without permission is about reclaiming authorship over your life. It is about recognizing that while you may not control every condition you face, you do control how you engage with those conditions. It is about choosing to live with clarity, discipline, and purpose, even when the external markers of success are still in development.

When you stop waiting for permission, you stop postponing your life. And in that moment, you begin to experience a form of richness that cannot be delayed, denied, or taken away.

CHAPTER THREE

The Psychology of Rich Living

Before wealth ever appears in a bank account, it is established in the mind. Not as fantasy or empty affirmation, but as a pattern of thought that governs perception, decision-making, and behavior. The way you interpret your circumstances, the meaning you assign to your experiences, and the expectations you hold for your life all contribute to a psychological framework that either expands or restricts what feels possible.

Most people underestimate how deeply their thinking is conditioned by repeated exposure to scarcity-based narratives. These narratives are reinforced through environment, conversation, media, and lived experience, gradually shaping a worldview in which limitation feels natural and abundance feels distant or unrealistic. Over time, this conditioning becomes so familiar that it is rarely questioned. It simply operates in the background, influencing choices without drawing attention to itself.

Scarcity thinking is not always loud or dramatic. It often presents as subtle assumptions: the belief that opportunities are limited, that success is reserved for others, or that effort will not produce meaningful change. These assumptions create a feedback loop in which hesitation replaces action, and inaction reinforces the original belief. The result is not a lack of potential, but a lack of engagement with that potential.

Rich living, in contrast, begins with a different psychological orientation. It is rooted in the understanding that while not all outcomes are guaranteed, the capacity to grow, adapt, and create value is always present. This perspective does not ignore challenges, but it refuses to treat them as final. Instead, it frames them as variables within a larger process, allowing for movement rather than stagnation.

One of the most important aspects of this shift is the way you relate to uncertainty. In a scarcity mindset, uncertainty is often interpreted as risk to be avoided. It represents the possibility of failure, loss, or disappointment, and therefore encourages caution to the point of paralysis. In a richer psychological framework, uncertainty is recognized as an inherent part of growth. It becomes something to navigate rather than something to fear, opening the door to experimentation, learning, and progress.

This change in perspective has a direct impact on how you approach decisions. When you are operating from a place of perceived lack, decisions tend to be reactive. They are driven by immediate concerns, short-term relief, or the desire to minimize discomfort. While this approach may provide temporary stability, it rarely leads to meaningful advancement. In contrast, when your thinking is grounded in a sense of possibility, decisions become more intentional. You begin to consider long-term impact, alignment with your values, and the potential for growth, even if the outcome is not guaranteed.

Another critical component of the psychology of rich living is self-perception. The way you see yourself influences how you show up in every area of your life. If you view yourself as limited, undeserving, or incapable, that perception will shape your actions in ways that reinforce those beliefs. You may hesitate to pursue opportunities, downplay your abilities, or accept conditions that do not reflect your true worth. Over time, this creates a pattern in which your external reality mirrors your internal narrative.

Shifting this dynamic requires more than positive thinking. It requires a deliberate effort to observe and challenge the assumptions that underpin your self-image. This involves paying attention to the language you use when you think about yourself, the expectations you set, and the standards you uphold. It also involves recognizing where you have unconsciously accepted limitations that no longer serve you, and choosing to replace them with a more accurate and constructive understanding of your capabilities.

Emotional regulation plays an equally significant role in this process. The ability to manage your emotional responses, particularly in the face of setbacks or uncertainty, directly influences your capacity to maintain forward momentum. Without this stability, even small challenges can feel overwhelming, leading to avoidance or withdrawal. When you develop the ability to remain grounded, you create space to respond thoughtfully rather than react impulsively, allowing you to navigate difficulties with greater clarity.

It is also important to acknowledge the role of comparison in shaping your psychological landscape. Constant exposure to curated representations of other people's lives can distort your perception of what is normal or attainable. When you measure your progress against incomplete or exaggerated benchmarks, it becomes easy to feel inadequate, regardless of your actual circumstances. This dynamic reinforces a sense of lack, making it more difficult to recognize and build upon what you already have.

Rich living requires a shift away from comparison and toward self-referenced growth. Instead of evaluating your progress based on external standards, you begin to measure it against your own development. This allows you to recognize improvement, build confidence, and maintain motivation without becoming dependent on validation from others. It also creates a more stable foundation for growth, as your sense of progress is no longer tied to variables outside your control.

Over time, these psychological adjustments begin to influence your behavior in consistent and measurable ways. You become more proactive, more resilient, and more aligned in your actions. Opportunities that once felt out of reach begin to feel accessible, not because circumstances have dramatically changed, but because your approach to them has. You are no longer constrained by assumptions that limit your engagement with the world.

The psychology of rich living is not about denying difficulty or pretending that challenges do not exist. It is about developing a framework that allows you to move through those challenges without losing your sense of direction or possibility. It is about recognizing that while external conditions may fluctuate, your internal orientation can remain stable, providing a reliable foundation for growth.

As this way of thinking becomes more integrated, it begins to shape not only how you experience your current life, but how you build your future. Decisions become more intentional, actions more consistent, and outcomes more aligned with your evolving sense of purpose. What once felt distant begins to feel attainable, not because it was out of reach, but because your perspective has expanded to meet it.

In this way, rich living is as much a psychological practice as it is a practical one. It is the ongoing process of aligning your thoughts, emotions, and actions with a standard that reflects possibility rather than limitation. And once that alignment is established, it becomes increasingly difficult to return to a way of thinking that confines you, because you have seen, with clarity, that a different way of living is not only possible — it is already within your reach.

CHAPTER FOUR

Standards Over Spending

One of the most overlooked truths about living well is that quality of life is far more influenced by standards than by spending. While money can certainly enhance comfort and expand options, it does not automatically elevate the way a person lives. Without clear standards, increased income often leads to increased consumption rather than increased fulfillment. The external appearance of wealth may improve, but the internal experience remains largely unchanged.

Standards operate differently. They are not dependent on income, nor are they limited by circumstance. They are decisions — quiet, consistent decisions — about what you will accept, what you will allow, and what you will require from yourself and your environment. Unlike spending, which fluctuates based on available resources, standards remain stable. They shape behavior regardless of financial condition, creating a continuity that allows for a more grounded and intentional way of living.

When standards are absent or unclear, spending often becomes a substitute for discernment. People attempt to compensate for a lack of clarity by acquiring more, believing that accumulation will create a sense of order or satisfaction. However, without a guiding framework, these acquisitions rarely align with what is genuinely valuable. Instead, they contribute to clutter — physical, mental, and emotional — making life feel more complicated rather than more refined.

Establishing standards begins with attention. It requires you to observe your current patterns without judgment, identifying where your choices reflect intention and where they are driven by habit or convenience. This process is not about criticism, but about awareness. It allows you to see where your actions are aligned with the life you want to create and where they are not, providing a foundation for more deliberate decision-making.

One of the first areas where standards become visible is in your immediate environment. The condition of your space influences your mental clarity, your energy, and your overall sense of stability. When your surroundings are disorganized or neglected, it creates a subtle but persistent friction that affects how you move through your day. In contrast, a clean, orderly environment supports focus and calm, making it easier to engage with your responsibilities and priorities.

Maintaining such an environment does not require significant financial investment. It requires consistency and care. It involves making small, deliberate choices — returning items to their place, minimizing unnecessary possessions, and creating a space that reflects how you want to feel rather than what you have accumulated. These actions, while simple, establish a standard that reinforces self-respect and intentionality.

Standards also influence how you manage your time. Without them, time is often allocated reactively, shaped by external demands, distractions, and immediate impulses. Hours are spent in ways that do not contribute to growth or fulfillment, leaving a sense of dissatisfaction that is difficult to articulate. When you establish clear standards for how your time is used, you create a structure that prioritizes what is meaningful, reducing the likelihood of drift and distraction.

This does not mean that every moment must be optimized or rigidly controlled. Rather, it involves making conscious decisions about where your attention is directed, ensuring that your time reflects your values rather than your impulses. Over time, this approach creates a rhythm that supports both productivity and rest, allowing for a more balanced and sustainable way of living.

The concept of standards extends beyond environment and time into the realm of personal conduct. How you speak, how you present yourself, and how you interact with others all contribute to the overall quality of your life. These elements are often underestimated because they do not carry a direct financial cost, yet they have a significant impact on both self-perception and external perception.

When you hold yourself to a higher standard in these areas, you create a sense of alignment between who you are and how you move through the world. This alignment fosters confidence, not as a performance, but as a natural outcome of consistency. You begin to trust your own behavior, knowing that it reflects a deliberate choice rather than a reaction to circumstance.

It is important to recognize that standards are not about perfection. They are not rigid rules that leave no room for flexibility or growth. Instead, they are guiding principles that provide direction while allowing for adaptation. As your understanding evolves, your standards can evolve with you, becoming more refined and more closely aligned with your values.

One of the challenges in maintaining standards is the influence of external environments that do not reflect the same level of intentionality. It is not always possible to control the spaces you enter or the people you encounter. However, it is always possible to control how you respond. By maintaining your standards regardless of external conditions, you create a sense of internal stability that is not easily disrupted.

Over time, the consistent application of standards begins to shape your experience in tangible ways. Your environment becomes more supportive, your time more purposeful, and your interactions more meaningful. These changes may not be immediately dramatic, but they accumulate, gradually transforming the quality of your life.

In contrast, reliance on spending alone rarely produces lasting change. While it can provide temporary satisfaction, it does not address the underlying patterns that determine how you live. Without standards, increased resources often lead to increased complexity rather than increased clarity, making it more difficult to sustain a sense of richness.

Living rich, therefore, is not about how much you can afford, but about how well you choose to live within your means. It is about establishing standards that reflect your values and applying them consistently, regardless of circumstance. When you prioritize standards over spending, you create a framework that supports a richer, more intentional life — one that is not dependent on financial milestones, but grounded in deliberate choice.

And in that framework, wealth begins to take on a different meaning. It is no longer defined by accumulation, but by alignment.

CHAPTER FIVE

Curating a Rich Environment

The environments in which people live and move are rarely neutral. They either support clarity, focus, and well-being, or they quietly erode them over time. While this influence is often subtle, it is persistent, shaping mood, behavior, and even self-perception in ways that are not always immediately recognized. For this reason, the act of curating one's environment is not superficial; it is foundational to the experience of living well.

Many people associate a refined or "rich" environment with high cost, imagining that beauty, order, and comfort require significant financial investment. This assumption leads to a form of passive neglect, where spaces are tolerated rather than shaped, and where the condition of one's surroundings is seen as an inevitable reflection of financial limitation. In reality, the quality of an environment is far more dependent on attention and intention than on expense. A thoughtfully arranged space, even with modest resources, can create a sense of calm and dignity that is often absent in more costly but neglected surroundings.

The process of curation begins with awareness. It requires an honest assessment of what your environment currently communicates, both visually and emotionally. Every object, every arrangement, and every level of organization contributes to an overall atmosphere. When a space is cluttered or chaotic, it generates a low-grade tension that affects concentration and emotional ease. Conversely, when a space is orderly and intentional, it provides a sense of stability that supports both rest and productivity.

One of the most effective ways to begin this process is through subtraction rather than addition. There is a natural tendency to believe that improvement requires acquiring more, yet in many cases, the opposite is true. Removing items that are unnecessary, unused, or misaligned with your current needs creates space — both physically and mentally. This space allows what remains to be seen more clearly and appreciated more fully, reducing the sense of overwhelm that often accompanies excess.

Once unnecessary elements are removed, attention can be directed toward arrangement. How items are placed within a space influences not only its functionality but also its emotional tone. Simple adjustments — such as ensuring that frequently used items are easily accessible, that surfaces are clear, and that visual clutter is minimized — can significantly improve how a space is experienced. These changes do not require additional resources, only a willingness to engage thoughtfully with what is already present.

Sensory elements also play a crucial role in shaping environment. Light, sound, and even scent contribute to the overall atmosphere, often in ways that are felt more than consciously noticed. Natural light, when available, can enhance mood and energy, while softer, controlled lighting can create a sense of calm in the evening. Sound, whether through music, silence, or ambient noise, influences focus and emotional state. Even subtle choices, such as maintaining a fresh and clean scent, can reinforce a sense of care and attentiveness.

Beyond the physical space, it is important to consider the informational environment you inhabit. The content you consume — whether through media, conversation, or digital platforms — has a direct impact on your thinking and emotional state. Constant exposure to negativity, distraction, or superficial comparison can create an internal environment that feels cluttered and unsettled. Curating this aspect of your environment involves being selective about what you engage with, prioritizing inputs that inform, inspire, or contribute to your growth.

This level of intentionality extends to the people with whom you spend time. Relationships are a significant component of environment, shaping not only how you feel but also how you see yourself. When you are surrounded by individuals who support your growth, respect your boundaries, and engage with you in meaningful ways, it reinforces a sense of value and possibility. Conversely, environments characterized by negativity, inconsistency, or lack of respect can diminish your sense of stability, regardless of other conditions.

It is not always possible to change every aspect of your external environment immediately. Circumstances such as shared spaces, work conditions, or financial constraints may limit your options. However, even within these limitations, there are always areas where you can exercise control. A single corner of a room, a daily routine, or a boundary in a relationship can serve as a starting point. These small areas of intentionality, when maintained consistently, begin to influence the larger environment over time.

Curating a rich environment also requires an understanding that maintenance is an ongoing process rather than a one-time effort. Without regular attention, even the most carefully arranged space can gradually return to disorder. Developing simple, consistent habits — such as tidying at the end of the day, reassessing what you keep, and making small adjustments as needed — ensures that your environment continues to support rather than hinder your experience.

As this practice becomes integrated into your daily life, the effects become increasingly noticeable. You may find that you are able to focus more easily, that your mood remains more stable, and that you approach your responsibilities with greater clarity. These changes are not the result of dramatic transformation, but of sustained attention to the details that shape your surroundings.

In this way, environment becomes an extension of your standards. It reflects not what you can afford, but what you choose to prioritize. When you approach your space with intention, you create a setting that supports a richer way of living, regardless of external circumstances.

Ultimately, curating a rich environment is an act of self-respect. It is a recognition that the spaces you occupy influence the life you experience, and that you have both the ability and the responsibility to shape those spaces in ways that align with your values. Through this process, richness becomes not something you acquire, but something you cultivate — quietly, consistently, and with purpose.

CHAPTER SIX

Time: The Currency You Keep Wasting

There is a peculiar contradiction in the way most people relate to time. While it is universally acknowledged as valuable, it is rarely treated with the same level of care as money.

People track their spending, monitor their accounts, and make deliberate decisions about financial resources, yet they allow hours of their lives to pass with little awareness of how they are being used.

This imbalance creates a quiet but significant loss, one that accumulates over time without the immediate visibility that accompanies financial depletion.

Time, unlike money, cannot be recovered once it is spent. It does not offer refunds, extensions, or second chances in the way financial systems sometimes do. Each day presents a finite number of hours, and how those hours are used shapes not only immediate outcomes but the trajectory of one's life.

Despite this, time is often treated as though it were abundant, leading to patterns of use that do not reflect its true value.

One of the primary reasons for this disconnect is the absence of structure. Without a clear framework for how time is allocated, it becomes vulnerable to external demands and internal impulses. Notifications, conversations, and distractions fill the available space, creating a sense of busyness that is often mistaken for productivity. In reality, much of this activity lacks direction, contributing little to meaningful progress or fulfillment.

The experience of being constantly occupied without feeling accomplished is a common indicator that time is not being used intentionally. It suggests that attention is being fragmented, moving from one task or distraction to another without a cohesive plan.

This fragmentation reduces the quality of engagement, making even simple tasks feel more taxing than they need to be. Over time, it leads to a sense of fatigue that is not necessarily the result of effort, but of inefficiency.

Reclaiming time begins with awareness, much like any other form of resource management. It requires an honest assessment of how your hours are currently spent, identifying patterns that contribute to growth and those that do not.

This process is not about assigning blame, but about gaining clarity. When you see where your time is going, you are better positioned to make adjustments that align with your priorities.

One of the most effective ways to introduce structure is through intentional planning. This does not require rigid scheduling of every moment, but it does involve setting clear expectations for how key portions of your time will be used. By identifying periods for focused work, rest, and personal development, you create a framework that reduces the likelihood of drift. Within this framework, there is still room for flexibility, but that flexibility exists within a context of purpose rather than absence of direction.

It is also important to recognize the role of boundaries in protecting your time. Without boundaries, time becomes easily accessible to others, often at the expense of your own priorities. Requests, interruptions, and obligations can accumulate, leaving little space for what is personally meaningful.

Establishing boundaries is not about withdrawing from responsibility, but about ensuring that your time reflects your values rather than solely the expectations of others.

This requires a willingness to say no when necessary, as well as the ability to communicate your limits clearly. While this may feel uncomfortable initially, it is essential for maintaining control over how your time is used. Over time, these boundaries create a more balanced distribution of attention, allowing you to engage more fully with the commitments you choose to accept.

Another aspect of time management that is often overlooked is the importance of rest. In a culture that frequently equates productivity with constant activity, rest is sometimes viewed as unproductive or indulgent. However, without adequate rest, the quality of both thought and action declines. Fatigue impairs decision-making, reduces focus, and increases the likelihood of errors, ultimately making tasks take longer and require more effort.

Rest, when approached intentionally, becomes a component of productivity rather than a departure from it. It allows for recovery, reflection, and the consolidation of learning, all of which contribute to more effective use of time in the long term. This includes not only sleep, but also periods of mental disengagement, where attention is allowed to shift away from structured tasks.

The way you begin and end your day also has a significant impact on how time is experienced. Mornings set the tone, influencing your level of focus and direction, while evenings provide an opportunity to reflect and reset.

When these transitional periods are approached with intention, they create a sense of continuity that supports more effective use of the hours in between.

Technology, while offering convenience and connectivity, presents another challenge in the management of time. The constant availability of information and entertainment makes it easy to fill any moment of stillness with stimulation. While this can provide short-term engagement,

it often comes at the cost of deeper focus and sustained attention. Being selective about how and when you engage with technology is essential for preserving the quality of your time.

As you begin to treat time with the same level of respect as money, your relationship with it changes. You become more deliberate in your choices, more aware of how your actions align with your goals, and more capable of creating a rhythm that supports both productivity and well-being. This shift does not require perfection, but it does require consistency.

Over time, the cumulative effect of these changes becomes evident. Tasks are completed with greater efficiency, goals are pursued with clearer direction, and the sense of being overwhelmed begins to diminish. You start to experience your days as structured yet flexible, purposeful yet manageable.

In this way, time reveals itself as a form of wealth that is available to everyone, yet fully utilized by few. It is a resource that, when managed with intention, has the capacity to transform not only what you accomplish, but how you experience your life. By recognizing its value and choosing to use it deliberately, you begin to live in a way that reflects richness — not because of what you have accumulated, but because of how you have chosen to spend what cannot be replaced.

CHAPTER SEVEN

The Discipline of Desire

Desire is often misunderstood. It is frequently treated as something to be indulged without question or suppressed without examination, depending on one's circumstances and conditioning. In the context of limited financial resources, desire can become particularly complicated. It may feel like a reminder of what is out of reach, or conversely, a justification for decisions that offer immediate satisfaction but undermine long-term stability. In either case, when desire operates without discipline, it tends to create imbalance rather than fulfillment.

At its core, desire is not the problem. It is a natural and necessary part of human experience, signaling what we are drawn to, what we value, and what we aspire toward. The issue arises when desire is left unexamined, when it is allowed to dictate behavior without consideration of consequence or alignment. In such cases, it becomes reactive, shaped by impulse, comparison, and external influence rather than internal clarity.

The discipline of desire begins with awareness. It requires you to pause long enough to understand what you want and why you want it. This distinction is essential because not all desires originate from the same place. Some are rooted in genuine interest or need, while others are influenced by social pressure, advertising, or the desire to signal status. Without examining the source, it is easy to pursue things that do not contribute to your well-being, mistaking momentary excitement for lasting value.

One of the most significant challenges in managing desire is the culture of immediacy in which many people operate. The expectation that satisfaction should be instant has been reinforced by technology, convenience, and accessibility. With a few clicks or a brief search, many desires can be acted upon almost immediately, reducing the time between wanting and having. While this can be beneficial in certain contexts, it often diminishes the ability to evaluate whether a desire is worth pursuing.

Introducing a pause between desire and action is a powerful practice. This pause creates space for reflection, allowing you to assess whether what you want aligns with your priorities and whether it contributes to the kind of life you are building. It transforms desire from a command into a consideration, shifting your role from passive responder to active decision-maker.

This process also involves distinguishing between temporary urges and enduring preferences. Temporary urges are often driven by emotion or circumstance. They arise quickly and can feel compelling in the moment, but they tend to fade just as rapidly. Enduring preferences, on the other hand, reflect deeper values and remain consistent over time. Learning to recognize this difference helps prevent decisions that are later regretted, particularly when resources are limited.

Financial discipline is closely tied to this ability. When spending is guided by impulse, it often leads to patterns that are difficult to sustain. Small, frequent decisions accumulate, gradually affecting financial stability without any single action appearing significant on its own. By applying discipline to desire, you create a filter that ensures your resources are directed toward what genuinely matters, rather than what simply captures your attention in the moment.

It is important to note that discipline is not synonymous with deprivation. It does not require you to eliminate enjoyment or deny yourself entirely. Instead, it encourages intentionality. It allows you to experience satisfaction more fully because your choices are aligned with your values. When you choose deliberately, rather than react impulsively, the outcome carries a different weight. It feels earned, considered, and integrated into your broader sense of purpose.

The discipline of desire also extends beyond financial decisions into how you allocate your time and energy. Just as with spending, there are countless ways to engage your attention, many of which offer immediate gratification but little long-term benefit. Without discipline, it is easy to become consumed by activities that provide temporary relief or distraction, while neglecting those that contribute to growth and fulfillment.

Developing this discipline requires consistency. It is not established through a single decision, but through repeated practice. Each time you pause, reflect, and choose intentionally, you reinforce a pattern that becomes easier to maintain over time. This does not mean that every decision will be perfect, but it does mean that your overall direction becomes more aligned with your priorities.

There is also a deeper psychological component to this process. When you demonstrate the ability to manage your desires, you build a sense of trust in yourself. You begin to see that you are capable of making decisions that serve your long-term interests, even when short-term temptations are present. This trust strengthens your confidence, not as an abstract feeling, but as a result of consistent behavior.

Over time, this shift changes your relationship with desire itself. Instead of viewing it as something that must be satisfied immediately, you begin to see it as information. It becomes a signal that can be interpreted, evaluated, and acted upon with intention. This perspective allows you to engage with your desires in a way that is both responsive and controlled, creating a balance between enjoyment and discipline.

In the context of living rich without significant financial resources, this balance is essential. It ensures that your pursuit of a fulfilling life is not undermined by choices that create unnecessary strain or instability. It allows you to direct your energy and resources toward what truly enhances your experience, rather than dispersing them across a range of impulses that do not contribute to your overall well-being.

Ultimately, the discipline of desire is about alignment. It is about ensuring that what you pursue reflects who you are becoming, rather than who you are reacting as. It is a practice that requires attention, patience, and consistency, but its impact extends far beyond individual decisions. It shapes the way you live, the way you experience satisfaction, and the way you build a life that feels both intentional and rich.

And in that alignment, desire no longer controls you. It informs you.

CHAPTER EIGHT

Relationships That Feel Like Wealth

There are forms of wealth that cannot be stored, counted, or displayed, yet their presence — or absence — shapes the entire experience of a person's life. Relationships belong to this category. They function as an invisible infrastructure, supporting emotional stability, influencing decision-making, and contributing to a sense of belonging that no amount of financial success can replace. When relationships are strong, life feels anchored. When they are strained, superficial, or absent, even the most materially comfortable circumstances can feel hollow.

Despite their importance, relationships are often approached with far less intention than other areas of life. People invest time and energy into building careers, managing finances, and acquiring possessions, yet they allow their connections with others to develop passively.

They tolerate dynamics that drain them, maintain interactions that lack depth, and avoid the effort required to cultivate meaningful bonds. Over time, this approach results in a network of relationships that may be extensive, but not enriching.

To understand relationships as a form of wealth requires a shift in perspective. It means recognizing that the value of a relationship is not determined by its visibility, its convenience, or its longevity, but by its quality. A single relationship characterized by mutual respect, honesty, and support can contribute more to a person's sense of well-being than dozens of superficial connections. Quality, in this context, is defined by the degree to which a relationship allows both individuals to be seen, understood, and supported without the need for constant performance or pretense.

One of the foundational elements of such relationships is presence. In an environment where attention is frequently divided, the act of being fully present with another person has become increasingly rare. Conversations are interrupted by notifications, interactions are filtered through distraction, and listening is often replaced by waiting for an opportunity to respond. This pattern diminishes the depth of connection, creating interactions that feel incomplete, even when they are frequent.

Cultivating presence requires intentional effort. It involves setting aside distractions, engaging with genuine curiosity, and allowing space for the other person to express themselves fully.

When presence is established, communication becomes more meaningful, and the relationship begins to develop a sense of depth that cannot be replicated through surface-level interaction. This depth is what transforms a relationship from an obligation into a source of enrichment.

Trust is another critical component, and it is built through consistency rather than grand gestures. It develops over time as individuals demonstrate reliability, honesty, and respect in both small and significant ways. When trust is present, it creates a sense of security that allows for vulnerability. Without it, relationships remain guarded, limiting the extent to which they can provide genuine support or understanding.

It is also important to consider the role of boundaries in maintaining the quality of relationships. Boundaries are often misunderstood as barriers, when in reality, they are structures that preserve respect and balance. Without clear boundaries, relationships can become imbalanced, with one person's needs or behaviors overshadowing the other's. This imbalance leads to resentment, fatigue, and eventual disconnection.

Establishing boundaries requires clarity about what you are willing to accept and what you are not. It involves communicating these limits in a way that is both firm and respectful, ensuring that the relationship operates within a framework that supports both individuals. While this process may initially feel uncomfortable, it ultimately strengthens the relationship by creating conditions in which both parties can engage authentically.

In the context of living rich without significant financial resources, relationships take on an even greater significance. They become sources of support, learning, and shared experience that do not rely on financial expenditure. A meaningful conversation, a shared meal, or a moment of genuine connection can provide a sense of richness that is independent of material conditions. These experiences, while simple, contribute to a life that feels full and grounded.

However, not all relationships contribute positively to this sense of richness. Some relationships are characterized by negativity, inconsistency, or lack of respect. They drain energy, create unnecessary stress, and reinforce limiting beliefs. Recognizing these dynamics is essential, as maintaining such relationships out of habit or obligation can undermine the very sense of well-being that rich living seeks to cultivate.

This recognition does not always require immediate or dramatic change. In some cases, it may involve adjusting the level of engagement, setting clearer boundaries, or redefining expectations. In others, it may require a more decisive shift, creating distance from relationships that consistently detract from your growth and stability. These decisions are not always easy, but they are necessary for preserving the quality of your relational environment.

Equally important is the role you play within your relationships. It is easy to focus on what others provide or fail to provide, but meaningful connections are inherently reciprocal. They require you to show up with the same level of presence, honesty, and respect that you expect from others. This involves listening actively, communicating clearly, and being willing to engage with both the strengths and challenges that arise within the relationship.

As you begin to approach relationships with greater intention, you may find that your social landscape shifts. Some connections may deepen, while others naturally fall away. This process is not a loss, but a refinement. It allows you to invest your time and energy in relationships that align with your values, creating a network of connections that genuinely supports your well-being.

Over time, these relationships contribute to a sense of stability that extends beyond individual interactions. They create an environment in which you feel understood, supported, and encouraged to grow. This environment, while intangible, has a profound impact on how you experience your life. It influences your confidence, your resilience, and your ability to navigate challenges with a sense of perspective.

There is also a cumulative effect to consider. Just as financial investments grow over time, so too do relationships. The effort you invest in building and maintaining meaningful connections compounds, creating a foundation of support that becomes increasingly valuable as life evolves. These relationships become sources of wisdom, comfort, and continuity, providing a sense of richness that is not easily disrupted by external circumstances.

Ultimately, relationships that feel like wealth are not defined by frequency or proximity, but by depth and quality. They are built through presence, sustained through trust, and protected by boundaries. They require effort, but the return on that effort is immeasurable. In a world where many forms of wealth are uncertain or fluctuating, these relationships offer a form of stability that is both enduring and deeply fulfilling.

When you begin to prioritize this level of connection, you discover that richness is not something you experience alone. It is something that is shared, reinforced, and expanded through the people you choose to bring into your life. And in that shared experience, wealth takes on a meaning that extends far beyond anything that can be quantified.

CHAPTER NINE

The Power of Enough

There is a quiet, often unexamined tension that exists in the pursuit of more. It is the sense that whatever is currently present is insufficient, that fulfillment lies just beyond the next acquisition, achievement, or milestone. This tension is reinforced by a culture that consistently equates growth with accumulation and progress with expansion. Within this framework, the idea of "enough" can feel counterintuitive, even limiting, as though it suggests settling rather than striving.

However, the concept of enough, when understood correctly, is not about limitation.

It is about clarity. It is the ability to recognize when your needs have been met, when your efforts have produced value, and when further pursuit is no longer driven by purpose but by habit or external pressure. Without this clarity, the pursuit of more becomes continuous, detached from any meaningful sense of completion. No matter how much is gained, it never feels sufficient, because the criteria for sufficiency have never been defined.

This lack of definition creates a cycle that is difficult to break. When enough is undefined, it is perpetually out of reach. Each achievement becomes a temporary point of satisfaction, quickly replaced by a new target. Over time, this pattern can lead to exhaustion, as the individual remains in a constant state of striving without experiencing the stability that comes from recognizing progress. The absence of a clear endpoint transforms growth into a perpetual chase rather than a purposeful journey.

Living rich without significant financial resources requires a different relationship with this dynamic. It requires the ability to identify and appreciate what is already present, without diminishing the value of future aspirations. This balance is delicate but essential. It allows for both contentment and ambition to coexist, preventing one from undermining the other.

The power of enough begins with awareness. It involves taking deliberate moments to assess your current circumstances, not through the lens of comparison, but through the lens of sufficiency. This means asking whether your basic needs are met, whether your environment supports your well-being, and whether your daily experiences contain elements of meaning and satisfaction. These questions are not designed to eliminate desire, but to ground it in reality.

When you recognize that certain aspects of your life are already sufficient, it creates a sense of stability. This stability reduces the urgency that often accompanies the pursuit of more, allowing you to make decisions from a place of intention rather than pressure. Instead of reacting to perceived lack, you begin to act based on clear priorities, directing your efforts toward areas that genuinely require attention.

Gratitude plays a significant role in this process, but it must be approached with depth rather than as a superficial exercise. Genuine gratitude is not about forcing positivity or ignoring challenges. It is about acknowledging the value of what exists, even within imperfect conditions. It requires a level of attention that allows you to see details that might otherwise be overlooked, transforming ordinary moments into sources of appreciation.

This shift in perception has a direct impact on how you experience your life. When you are able to identify and appreciate what is enough, you reduce the sense of scarcity that often drives unnecessary consumption. You become less inclined to seek validation through acquisition and more inclined to engage with what you already have. This does not eliminate the desire for improvement, but it ensures that such desire is grounded rather than compulsive.

It is also important to recognize that the concept of enough is not static. It evolves as your circumstances, priorities, and understanding change. What feels sufficient at one stage of life may not remain so at another. The key is not to fix a permanent definition, but to maintain an ongoing awareness of what is appropriate for your current context. This adaptability allows you to respond to change without losing your sense of balance.

In financial terms, the power of enough can influence how you approach both spending and saving. When you have a clear sense of what satisfies your needs and aligns with your values, you are less likely to engage in unnecessary expenditure. At the same time, you are more capable of directing resources toward areas that contribute to long-term stability. This creates a more sustainable relationship with money, one that is guided by purpose rather than impulse.

Beyond finances, the concept of enough extends to how you allocate your time and energy. Without a sense of sufficiency, it is easy to overcommit, filling your schedule with activities that do not contribute to your well-being. This often leads to fatigue and a diminished capacity to engage meaningfully with any single task. When you recognize what is enough, you are better able to set limits, ensuring that your commitments reflect your priorities.

There is also a psychological dimension to consider. The ability to accept enough challenges the internal narrative that equates worth with constant productivity or achievement. It allows you to separate your value from your output, creating space for rest, reflection, and enjoyment. This separation is essential for maintaining a sense of self that is not entirely dependent on external validation.

At the same time, embracing enough does not require abandoning ambition. It is entirely possible to pursue growth while maintaining a sense of contentment. The distinction lies in the motivation behind your actions. When ambition is driven by curiosity, purpose, or a desire to contribute, it tends to be sustainable and fulfilling. When it is driven by comparison or the need to prove something, it often leads to dissatisfaction, regardless of the outcome.

Over time, the practice of recognizing enough reshapes your relationship with both success and failure. Success is no longer measured solely by accumulation, but by alignment with your values and satisfaction with your experiences. Failure, in turn, becomes less threatening, as it does not undermine your sense of sufficiency. You are able to view it as part of a broader process rather than as a definitive statement about your worth.

In this way, the power of enough becomes a stabilizing force. It provides a reference point that allows you to navigate change without losing perspective. It enables you to appreciate what is present while remaining open to what is possible, creating a balance that supports both well-being and growth.

Ultimately, living rich is not about eliminating the desire for more, but about ensuring that the pursuit of more does not prevent you from recognizing the value of what you already have. When you understand what is enough, you free yourself from the endless cycle of dissatisfaction, creating space for a life that feels both complete and continually evolving.

CHAPTER TEN

Living Ahead of Your Circumstances

There is a difference between denying reality and refusing to be defined by it. The former is rooted in avoidance, while the latter is grounded in intention. Living ahead of your circumstances requires the ability to see your current condition clearly while choosing not to let it dictate the full scope of your behavior, your standards, or your expectations for your life. It is not an act of illusion, but an act of alignment with the direction in which you are moving.

Many people anchor their behavior to their present situation, allowing it to determine how they think, speak, and act. If resources are limited, they shrink their standards. If opportunities appear scarce, they lower their expectations. If progress feels slow, they reduce their effort. This approach creates a feedback loop in which current conditions are continuously reinforced, making it difficult to create meaningful change. When behavior is consistently aligned with limitation, limitation tends to persist.

Living ahead of your circumstances disrupts this pattern. It involves aligning your actions with the person you are becoming rather than the position you currently occupy. This alignment is not based on pretense, but on preparation. It reflects a decision to embody the habits, discipline, and mindset that will support your future, even before external conditions have fully caught up.

One of the most visible ways this principle manifests is in personal standards. When individuals choose to maintain a certain level of care in how they present themselves, organize their environment, and manage their responsibilities, regardless of financial condition, they create continuity between their present and their future. These standards are not dependent on excess resources; they are expressions of identity. They signal a commitment to living with intention rather than reacting to circumstance.

This approach also influences how you make decisions. Instead of asking what is easiest or most convenient in the moment, you begin to consider what aligns with your long-term direction. This shift does not eliminate practical constraints, but it changes how those constraints are navigated. You become more deliberate, weighing choices against a broader context rather than immediate relief. Over time, this leads to decisions that support growth, even when they require more effort or patience.

Language plays a significant role in this process. The way you speak about your situation, both internally and externally, shapes how you experience it. When your language is rooted in limitation, it reinforces a sense of restriction. When it is grounded in possibility, it creates space for movement. This does not mean ignoring challenges, but it does mean framing them in a way that allows for progress. Words such as "currently" and "in this season" acknowledge reality without assigning permanence to it.

Another important aspect of living ahead of your circumstances is the way you engage with opportunity. Opportunities are not always obvious, and they rarely present themselves in ideal form. They often require recognition, interpretation, and action. When you are anchored solely in your present condition, it is easy to overlook these possibilities, dismissing them as irrelevant or unattainable. When you are oriented toward your future, you are more likely to recognize and engage with opportunities, even if they require effort to develop.

This perspective also affects how you approach learning and skill development. Instead of waiting until conditions are favorable, you begin to invest in your growth with the resources available to you. This may involve self-directed learning, practice, or seeking out experiences that expand your capabilities. Each step, while perhaps small in isolation, contributes to a larger trajectory of development that positions you for future advancement.

There is, however, a balance that must be maintained. Living ahead of your circumstances does not require you to overextend yourself financially or to engage in behavior that creates unnecessary strain. It is not about attempting to replicate a lifestyle that is not yet sustainable. Rather, it is about embodying the principles and habits that define that lifestyle, without relying on external markers to validate them. This distinction ensures that your actions remain grounded, even as your perspective expands.

Consistency is a critical factor in this process. Occasional alignment with your future self is not sufficient to create lasting change. It is the repeated application of these principles that produces momentum. Each time you choose discipline over convenience, intention over impulse, and alignment over reaction, you reinforce a pattern that becomes increasingly natural over time.

As this pattern develops, it begins to influence how others perceive and interact with you. While external validation is not the goal, it is often a byproduct of consistent behavior. People respond to clarity, reliability, and intention, and these qualities can create opportunities that might not have been accessible otherwise. This is not a guarantee, but it is a reflection of how internal alignment can extend outward.

It is also important to recognize that living ahead of your circumstances requires patience. External conditions do not always change at the same pace as internal development. There may be periods in which your habits, mindset, and efforts are well aligned with your future, yet your circumstances appear unchanged. During these periods, it is essential to maintain consistency, trusting that the alignment you are creating is building a foundation that will support future outcomes.

Over time, the gap between your current circumstances and your internal alignment begins to close. Opportunities become more accessible, decisions yield more favorable results, and your overall experience of life begins to reflect the standards you have established. This process is not instantaneous, but it is cumulative, with each aligned action contributing to a broader transformation.

Ultimately, living ahead of your circumstances is about ownership. It is about recognizing that while you may not control every aspect of your environment, you do control how you engage with it. It is about choosing to operate from a place of intention, even when conditions are less than ideal, and trusting that this alignment will influence your trajectory over time.

When you adopt this approach, your circumstances no longer define your limits. They become a starting point — one that you acknowledge, but do not allow to dictate the full extent of your life. And in that shift, you begin to experience a form of richness that is not dependent on where you are, but on how you choose to move forward.

CHAPTER ELEVEN

The Language of Abundance

Language is not merely a tool for communication; it is a framework through which reality is interpreted, organized, and reinforced. The words you use, both in conversation with others and in the private dialogue you maintain with yourself, shape how you perceive your circumstances and how you respond to them. Over time, this language becomes habitual, forming patterns that influence belief, behavior, and ultimately, experience.

For many people, especially those navigating financial limitation, the language they adopt is rooted in scarcity. It is reflected in phrases that emphasize restriction, lack, and impossibility. Statements such as "I can't afford that," "That's not for people like me," or "Maybe someday" may seem harmless in isolation, but when repeated consistently, they reinforce a narrative in which options are limited and progress is uncertain. This narrative does not simply describe reality; it begins to define it.

The impact of this language is subtle but significant. When you repeatedly articulate limitation, your mind begins to accept it as a fixed condition rather than a variable one. This acceptance influences how you approach decisions, often leading to hesitation, avoidance, or resignation. Opportunities that require initiative may be dismissed prematurely, and solutions that demand creativity may remain unexplored. In this way, language becomes both a reflection of perception and a contributor to its persistence.

Shifting toward a language of abundance does not require denying reality or ignoring practical constraints. Instead, it involves reframing how those constraints are understood and communicated. Rather than focusing solely on what is unavailable, this approach emphasizes possibility, resourcefulness, and direction. It acknowledges current limitations while maintaining openness to change, creating a more balanced and constructive perspective.

One of the most effective ways to begin this shift is by examining the automatic phrases that arise in your thinking. These phrases often operate below the level of conscious awareness, yet they carry significant influence. By bringing them into focus, you create an opportunity to evaluate their accuracy and usefulness. For example, replacing “I can’t afford that” with “That is not a priority for me right now” maintains the reality of the situation while removing the sense of helplessness. It reframes the decision as intentional rather than imposed.

This distinction is important because it preserves a sense of agency. When you speak in terms of choice rather than limitation, you reinforce the idea that you are actively managing your circumstances, even when resources are constrained. This perspective encourages engagement rather than withdrawal, making it more likely that you will seek out alternatives or develop strategies to move forward.

The language of abundance also influences how you approach problem-solving. When your internal dialogue is oriented toward possibility, you are more likely to ask constructive questions. Instead of concluding that something is unattainable, you begin to explore how it might be approached. Questions such as "What would it take to make this possible?" or "What is one step I can take in this direction?" shift your focus from limitation to action. They create a mental environment in which solutions are more likely to emerge.

It is equally important to consider the emotional tone of your language. Words carry not only meaning but also energy, influencing how you feel about your circumstances. Language that is consistently negative or defeatist can reinforce a sense of discouragement, making it more difficult to maintain motivation. In contrast, language that is grounded, constructive, and forward-looking supports a more stable emotional state, even in the presence of challenges.

This does not mean adopting exaggerated or unrealistic expressions of positivity. The goal is not to convince yourself that everything is ideal, but to communicate in a way that supports clarity and movement. For example, acknowledging that a situation is difficult while also recognizing that it is temporary allows you to remain grounded without becoming overwhelmed. This balanced approach ensures that your language remains both honest and constructive.

The influence of language extends beyond individual thought into interactions with others. The way you speak in conversations shapes not only how you are perceived, but also how those around you respond. Language that reflects confidence, intention, and possibility tends to invite engagement and support, while language that emphasizes limitation may discourage collaboration or opportunity. Over time, these patterns of interaction contribute to the environment in which you operate, reinforcing either expansion or constraint.

There is also a cumulative effect to consider. Each time you choose language that reflects agency and possibility, you reinforce a pattern that becomes more natural over time. This repetition gradually reshapes your internal narrative, making it easier to maintain a perspective that supports growth. Conversely, if scarcity-based language remains unchallenged, it continues to reinforce patterns of thought that limit engagement and initiative.

It is important to recognize that changing your language is not an instant transformation. It requires consistent attention and a willingness to interrupt established patterns. There will be moments when old habits resurface, particularly in situations of stress or uncertainty. The key is not to eliminate these moments entirely, but to recognize them quickly and adjust. Each correction reinforces your ability to maintain a more constructive framework.

As this practice becomes integrated, its effects begin to extend into other areas of your life. Decision-making becomes more intentional, problem-solving more effective, and emotional responses more balanced. You begin to experience your circumstances differently, not because they have changed immediately, but because your relationship with them has evolved.

Over time, the language of abundance contributes to a broader shift in identity. You no longer see yourself as someone constrained solely by external conditions, but as someone capable of navigating and influencing those conditions. This shift does not eliminate challenges, but it changes how they are approached, making them more manageable and less defining.

In the context of living rich without significant financial resources, this shift is particularly powerful. It allows you to engage with your life in a way that emphasizes possibility over limitation, creating a sense of richness that is not dependent on immediate financial change. Your words begin to reflect a standard that is aligned with growth, and that alignment influences both your actions and your outcomes.

Ultimately, the language you use is a form of practice. It is a daily, ongoing expression of how you choose to interpret your experience. When that language is grounded in clarity, agency, and possibility, it creates a framework that supports a richer way of living — one that is not confined by circumstance, but shaped by intention.

CHAPTER TWELVE

Becoming The Asset

At a certain point in the pursuit of a richer life, attention must shift from external acquisition to internal development. Up to this stage, much of the focus has been on how you think, how you spend your time, how you manage your environment, and how you relate to others. Each of these areas contributes to the quality of your life, yet they all point toward a central truth that cannot be overlooked: the most valuable resource you will ever have is yourself.

To become the asset is to recognize that your skills, your discipline, your perception, and your ability to create value are not secondary to wealth — they are its foundation. Money, opportunities, and access are often byproducts of these internal qualities rather than their source. When you invest in yourself deliberately and consistently, you develop a form of value that is portable, adaptable, and not easily diminished by changing circumstances.

Many people, however, are conditioned to prioritize external validation over internal development. They focus on acquiring credentials, recognition, or material indicators of success, often without cultivating the underlying capabilities that sustain those achievements. This imbalance can create a fragile sense of stability, where success is dependent on conditions that are not fully within one's control. When those conditions shift, the absence of a strong internal foundation becomes apparent.

Becoming the asset requires a reversal of this pattern. It involves placing primary emphasis on the development of qualities that remain with you regardless of external change. These qualities include the ability to learn, to adapt, to think critically, and to act with consistency. They are not developed through occasional effort, but through sustained practice, reinforced over time.

One of the most significant aspects of this process is the cultivation of skill. Skills represent the practical application of knowledge, allowing you to create value in tangible ways. Unlike abstract understanding, which may remain unused, skills are inherently functional. They can be applied across contexts, refined through experience, and expanded as your capacity grows. In a world where conditions are constantly evolving, the ability to develop and adapt skills becomes a critical factor in maintaining relevance and opportunity.

The development of skill is closely tied to the willingness to engage in deliberate practice. This involves moving beyond passive consumption of information and actively applying what you learn. It requires patience, as progress is often incremental rather than immediate. It also requires resilience, as mistakes and setbacks are an inevitable part of the process. However, each instance of effort contributes to a cumulative effect, gradually increasing your capability and confidence.

Equally important is the cultivation of discipline. While motivation can initiate action, it is discipline that sustains it. Discipline is the ability to act consistently in alignment with your priorities, even when external conditions are not ideal. It allows you to maintain progress in the absence of immediate reward, reinforcing habits that support long-term development.

This consistency is particularly valuable when resources are limited. In such circumstances, the margin for error is often smaller, making it essential to use time and energy effectively. Discipline ensures that your efforts are directed toward meaningful objectives, reducing the likelihood of distraction or misalignment. Over time, this focused approach creates a level of efficiency that amplifies the impact of your actions.

Another critical component of becoming the asset is self-awareness. Understanding your strengths, your limitations, and your patterns of behavior allows you to make more informed decisions about where to focus your efforts. Without this awareness, it is easy to expend energy in areas that do not align with your capabilities or goals, leading to frustration and inefficiency.

Self-awareness also enables you to recognize areas for growth without attaching them to your sense of worth. This distinction is essential, as it allows you to approach development with clarity rather than defensiveness. You are able to identify what needs improvement and take action without interpreting it as a reflection of inadequacy. This mindset supports continuous growth, as it removes the resistance that often accompanies self-criticism.

In addition to skill and discipline, adaptability plays a significant role in sustaining your value. The ability to adjust to changing conditions, to learn new methods, and to respond effectively to uncertainty ensures that your capabilities remain relevant. In a dynamic environment, rigidity can limit opportunity, while adaptability creates flexibility. It allows you to navigate transitions with greater ease, maintaining momentum even when circumstances shift.

It is also important to consider the role of character in this process. Qualities such as integrity, reliability, and accountability contribute to how others perceive and interact with you. While these attributes may not always produce immediate, visible results, they build trust over time, creating opportunities that are often unavailable to those who lack consistency in these areas. Character, in this sense, becomes a form of long-term investment, yielding returns that extend beyond immediate transactions.

The process of becoming the asset is not confined to professional or financial contexts. It influences how you approach every aspect of your life, from relationships to personal development. When you see yourself as the primary source of value, you become more intentional in how you allocate your time, more selective in your commitments, and more focused in your efforts. This perspective creates a sense of ownership that extends beyond external conditions.

There is also a psychological shift that accompanies this process. When you recognize that your value is rooted in what you can develop and contribute, rather than what you currently possess, you reduce the anxiety associated with external fluctuation. Financial changes, while still significant, no longer carry the same weight, as they do not define your capacity to create or adapt. This creates a sense of stability that is grounded in your own capabilities.

Over time, the cumulative effect of these efforts becomes evident. Your skills expand, your discipline strengthens, and your ability to navigate complexity improves. Opportunities that once seemed distant become accessible, not because they have changed, but because you have. You are better prepared to recognize, pursue, and sustain them.

It is important to acknowledge that this process requires patience. The development of internal assets does not always produce immediate, visible results. There may be periods in which your efforts feel disproportionate to your outcomes. During these times, it is essential to maintain perspective, recognizing that growth often occurs beneath the surface before it becomes externally apparent.

Consistency, once again, is the determining factor. Each action, no matter how small, contributes to a broader pattern of development. Over time, these actions compound, creating a level of capability that distinguishes you from those who rely solely on external factors. This distinction is not always visible immediately, but it becomes increasingly apparent as opportunities arise and are either seized or missed.

Ultimately, becoming the asset is about reclaiming control over where value originates in your life. It shifts the focus from what you can acquire to what you can develop, from what is given to what is built. It establishes a foundation that is not easily disrupted by external change, allowing you to navigate uncertainty with greater confidence and clarity.

When you become the asset, you are no longer dependent on circumstance to define your potential. You carry that potential with you, applying it in ways that reflect your growth, your discipline, and your understanding. And in doing so, you create a form of wealth that is not only sustainable, but expandable — one that continues to grow as you do.

Conclusion

Everything I've Said, I've Lived

Everything I have written in this book is not theory. It is not something I studied from a distance or borrowed from someone else's life and repackaged into something that sounds good. Everything I've said, I've lived — imperfectly at times, but consistently enough to know that this way of living is real, sustainable, and transformative.

Since relocating to Chicago from Dallas in 2010, my journey has not been one of steady, predictable income. In fact, when I look back honestly, I have only had the equivalent of about six years of consistent income during that entire span of time. The rest has been filled with the ups and downs that come with entrepreneurship, creativity, and the kind of life that does not follow a traditional path. There have been seasons of uncertainty, moments where things did not look the way people assume they should, and stretches where I had to rely on discipline, faith, and strategy more than anything else.

And yet, in the midst of that, I have still built a life that many people associate with wealth.

I have purchased two properties in Illinois — one, a Chicago home that has stood for more than one hundred years, full of character and history; the other, a large vacant corner lot in a completely different area, representing both vision and future possibility.

I have also begun developing my retirement property, “Antiqua,” in Mississippi — paying for it in cash, piece by piece, which is why the process has taken time and why I am still working to repair the storm damage that nearly ripped my place to shreds. Thankfully, I got a deal on a mobile home that I put on my property so now it has three buildings on it since the original house already has a storage shed on property.

Yes, this is a long way from the grand vision I have, but it is also heading in a direction better than what I had in mind. No, it’s not as pretty as I want it to be, but it’s paid off, I have a place of my own to sleep in that no one can force me out of, and I can even start a glamping park!

Believe you me: There is nothing glamorous about rebuilding after that kind of loss, but there is something deeply grounding about knowing that what you are building is yours, fully and completely, without debt attached to it.

At the same time, my life has never been reduced to survival.

I still volunteer in various places because giving is a part of who I am, not something I postpone until I "have more." I continue to create and release my books and music because expression is not optional for me — it is essential. I am actively learning artificial intelligence well enough to finally produce and release my movie, because growth does not stop just because circumstances are not perfect.

I travel when I want to travel, whether that means enjoying time in Palm Beach or taking a quick trip to Canada with my passport. I spend time with the people I love, nurturing relationships that matter. I maintain a fulfilling and active love life. I enjoy my life.

And yes, I enjoy beautiful things.

I have accumulated clothing, shoes, and accessories to the point where some still have tags on them. I have an entire room dedicated to what people often describe as a walk-in closet, complete with racks I acquired from a retail store that was going out of business.

When people see it, they often say it looks like a department store. To them, it signals wealth. To me, it represents intention, taste, and the ability to create an environment that reflects how I choose to live — regardless of what my bank account might say at any given moment.

Through it all, I continue to thank The Most High for every blessing and for protection, even in the face of challenges that could have easily taken me out or set me back permanently. There are things that have come against me — and still do — that people may never fully understand. But I am still here. I am still building. I am still living.

And I want to be clear about something.

I am not sharing any of this from a place of superiority. I am not on a high horse. This book is not about presenting myself as someone who has everything figured out or someone who is above the realities that others face. I am sharing this because people have looked at my life — how I move, what I do, how I live — and they ask me, often without hesitation, “Are you rich?” or they say, “You must be rich or something.”

And I always have to explain.

I tell them that I have a wealth of joyous talents. I tell them that I am rich in loving peace. I tell them that I thank God for blessing me to be able to do things that I once believed required millions of dollars in the bank. Because the truth is, even without consistent income, even while navigating the challenges that come with being an entrepreneur and, at times, what people would call a "starving artist,"

I have positioned myself to live a life where I can do what I want to do, when I want to do it — as long as I am willing to make it happen or invest in getting the help I need to make it happen.

That positioning did not happen by accident.

One of the most important principles I have lived by is this: I put back half of whatever income I receive. No matter how much or how little comes in, I honor that standard.

That discipline has allowed me to maintain a level of stability that is not always visible on the surface. It ensures that I have funds to handle what needs to be handled and that I remain in a position to continue ascending — even if an investment does not pan out or a stream of income slows down.

That is what living rich looks like in real life.

It is not always flashy. It is not always easy. But it is intentional, and it is powerful.

I still have faith that my time is coming in a greater way — that my cup will be filled and run over. But I am not waiting for that moment to begin living. I am not postponing my life until everything aligns perfectly. I am positioning myself now to live in a way that is grand, divine, and aligned with who I am becoming.

Because I understand something now that I did not fully understand before:

If you wait to live richly until you have everything, you may never truly experience it. But if you learn how to live richly now, with what you have, as you are, where you are — you create a life that expands naturally into both spiritual and material opulence.

And when that expansion comes, you will not only be able to obtain it — you will be ready to enjoy it.

That is the life I am building.

And if you have read this far, I believe it is the life you are capable of building too.

A Note of Thanks

Eternal Gratitude

Thank you! Thank you for choosing this book, for investing your time, your attention, and your openness into these pages.

In a world filled with noise, distraction, and endless options, your decision to sit with these words means more than you may realize.

My hope is that as you close this book, you don't simply walk away inspired — you walk away clear.

Clear about what a rich life truly means *for you.*

Take a moment, even now, to decide what makes up the life of your dreams. Not the version shaped by pressure, comparison, or expectation — but the one that genuinely reflects your desires, your peace, your joy, and your purpose. Then ask yourself these simple-yet-powerful questions:

1. How can I begin living that life with the money I have access to — or the money I am capable of generating right now?
2. What changes in perspective or actions can I make today that can assure each day I live is the best it can be?

Because the truth is, the shift does not begin when everything aligns. It begins the moment you decide to live differently —

with intention, creativity, and unwavering belief in what is possible for you.

I am deeply grateful that you allowed me to be a part of that shift.

If this book spoke to you, I invite you to explore more of my work. I write across multiple genres, each one designed to inspire, challenge, and elevate in its own way. Simply type **"Mylia Tiye Mal Jaza"** into Amazon and take a look at what resonates with you next. There is something waiting there for you.

And this is not the end — it's an introduction.

I look forward to the day we cross paths in real life, somewhere beautiful, somewhere intentional, somewhere aligned… raising a glass and toasting to the opulent lives we chose to live — long before the world gave us permission.

Until then, keep living richly.

With gratitude,

Mylia Tiye Mal Jaza

www.ingramcontent.com/pod-product-compliance
Lightning Source LLC
LaVergne TN
LVHW010918110826
845149LV00013B/2408

9783517385938